Children's Mini...

FAQ,

Frequently Asked Questions

and 100+ Great Answers

By Dave Ebeling and Jim Gimbel

with the Christian Education Specialists
Paul Berg
Dee Christopher
Dr. Dave Ebeling
Gloria Lessmann
Jason J. Scheler
Joseph M. Snyder
Duane Tweeten
Rev. Ronald W. Brusius
Betty L. Brusius
Sarah Sailer

Illustrated by Gordon Willman

CPH
Concordia Publishing House

Copyright © 1999 Concordia Publishing House
3558 S. Jefferson Avenue, St. Louis, MO 63118-3968
Manufactured in the United States of America

This publication is also available in braille and in large print for the visually impaired. Write to Library for the Blind, 1333 S. Kirkwood Rd., St. Louis, MO 63122-7295; or call 1-800-433-3954.

1   2   3   4   5   6   7   8   9   10   09   08   07   06   05   04   03   02   01   00

Contents

"What a great idea!"

The Concordia Christian Education Specialists often hear and say that phrase as they work with creative and effective folks involved in the ministry of the church. Pastors, youth and education workers, and volunteers on the front lines of ministry are sharing the love of Christ in wonderful and meaningful ways. God's name is praised when great ideas are implemented that increase the human effectiveness of the power of the Gospel.

This book is a collection of some of these great ideas encountered by the Specialists through experiences in many varied but wonderful Christian education settings around the church. Solomon said "there is nothing new under the sun." Most of these ideas are not radical, but proceed out of experience, a unique challenge, or an inspired vision produced by the strong desire to pass along the message of salvation through Jesus Christ. Many of these ideas are already in place in a few congregations and are worth sharing with others. Other ideas involve a slightly new twist or emphasis to a common or familiar practice. A few of these ideas were created just for this book, the result of enthusiastic hearts and creative brains storming together on the topic of children's ministry at a Christian education workshop.

The role of the Concordia Christian Education Specialists has been to represent the face of CPH and our educational expertise in practical and meaningful ways that encourage and foster the very best for Christ. Since the fall of 1997, Concordia's Christian Education Specialists have provided pastors, teachers, church leaders, and volunteers with ideas and resources for their tasks. This book captures some of the Specialists' enthusiasm for Christ and children. The Specialists hope to meet each reader sometime and hear your great ideas and adaptations of ministry for Christ's sake. Let us know what works ... and what can be done differently!

Jim Lohman,
DCE, Director of the Concordia
Publishing House Christian
Education Specialists program

Paul Berg
Dee Christopher
Dr. Dave Ebeling
Gloria Lessmann
Jason J. Scheler
Joseph M. Snyder
Duane Tweeten
Rev. Ronald W. Brusius
Betty L. Brusius
Sarah Sailer

For more information on the Christian Education Specialists, or to have one visit your area, contact CPH at 1-800-325-3040, ext.1147.

Question 1

What can a congregation do to retain volunteer teachers?

Start right

1 Provide teachers with a clear job description.

2 Team new teachers with veteran teachers until they feel comfortable.

3 Build relationships between teachers and the church staff (including the pastor). This can be accomplished by a retreat at a local bed and breakfast, a campout, an overnight lock-in at church, or a challenge activity like rock climbing or canoeing. Or sponsor a kickoff dessert party hosted by a loyal supporter of the Children's Ministries or a "retired" teacher.

4 Make sure teachers know where supplies, rooms, etc. are located.

5 Provide teachers with an engraved notepad to encourage note-taking during times of spiritual growth.

6 Provide teachers with a shirt embroidered with the church name and "Teaching Staff."

7 Provide teachers with daily devotional materials (e.g., *God in My Classroom, Today's Light, Teaching 101*).

8 Spend time in the classroom with teachers so you can provide immediate feedback.

9 Recruit many support people to help with small tasks, such as registration and snacks, so that teachers can concentrate on teaching.

10 Meet with teachers individually to give encouragement and affirmation, as well as to foster self-evaluation and accountability. Listen carefully to their ideas, hurts, and joys, then follow up as necessary.

Show Appreciation

Try some of these ideas to affirm and show appreciation for your volunteer Teachers of the Faith.

☺ Profile each Teacher of the Faith in the church newsletter or on a bulletin board.

☺ Give small gifts and gift certificates.

☺ Have parents, pastors, leaders, and kids write and send thank-you notes.

☺ Visit their classroom to show your appreciation in front of the class.

☺ Recognize their birthday, baptismal birthday, anniversary, and other special days.

☺ Recognize the years of service they have given.

☺ Throw an appreciation dinner for all Teachers of the Faith. An informal pizza dinner may be as effective as a formal meal, as long as fellowship time is built in.

☺ Make sure teachers have access to adequate supplies.

☺ Post teachers' name on their classroom door.

☺ Give teachers their own locked supply box or shelf.

☺ Give them some of their own space if they share a room (a shelf, a bulletin board).

☺ Offer a retreat for teachers.

☺ Train teachers in the skills they need.

☺ Buy the resource books they need.

☺ Don't overburden teachers with other responsibilities (like leading the Christmas service).

☺ Recognize and show appreciation for the spouse and family of the Teachers of the Faith.

☺ Avoid scheduling too many things that compete with Sunday school.

Monthly motivation

August—Provide quality, permanent name tags and door-mounted name plates for teachers.

September—Install teachers at worship services, have a family luncheon following.

October—Do something just for fun—a hayride, a bonfire, order pizza for teachers and their families after a worship service.

November—Give thank-you baskets with personally selected items.

December—Sponsor a shopping party for the teachers, with day care at church, transportation, and time for fellowship.

January—Allow your teachers to attend a teacher-training event.

February—Pass out chocolate tokens of affection.

March—Give green mints, a church shirt, or movie passes as a thank-you gift.

April—Arrange for a photographer to take class pictures; then give one to each teacher.

May—Arrange for substitute teachers and host a Board of Education-sponsored appreciation breakfast for the staff.

June—Send or deliver flowers to teachers at church or at home.

July—Have an education festival that includes a picnic or barbecue.

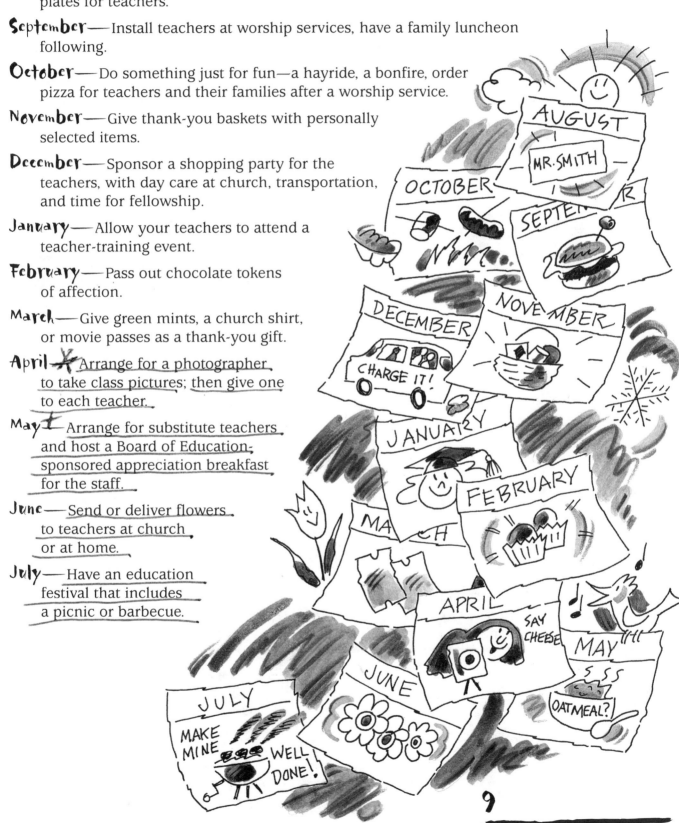

caught ya!

Catch 'em doing things right!

Each week, stop by a classroom during or immediately after class time to catch the teacher doing things right. Ask a few students for honest feedback on what they did and how the class went. Make the affirmation public; follow up with a fax, e-mail, or note card reinforcing what you saw and said. Make sure the affirmation is honest and meaningful.

use bulletin boards

Designate a prominent bulletin board for photos of your whole Teachers of the Faith staff, including the superintendent, teachers, helpers, the pastor, and others active in the ministry. The best photos will be candid shots showing interaction with students.

Have an idea box

Sometimes teachers want something to change but don't have the confidence or the private time to speak with a pastor or superintendent about it. Here are some tips of how to best benefit from the use of an "Idea" or "Suggestion" box:

Place it in an obvious location.

Allow anyone to submit a suggestion, including students and parents.

Encourage people to put their name and contact information on the note.

Make known the process of how suggestions are considered for implementation.

Recognize or reward those who suggest changes that are implemented. At minimum, publicize the suggested change and source; at best, reward people at a special ceremony for their contribution of ideas to Christ's ministry.

Establish a "Teachers of the Faith" supply store

Volunteer teachers often spend their time, money, and best efforts dedicated to children. Find a volunteer manager to set up and maintain a "Teachers of the Faith" supply store. Items in the store can be the ordinary educational supplies like scissors, crayons, writing paper, construction paper, tape, flannelgraph and characters, rulers, rubber stamps, glue, markers, pencils, Bibles, etc. A list of standard supplies can be provided for all the teachers, as well as a careful explanation of the checkout process. The well-stocked store can also include a large variety of costumes for drama and magazines for cutting apart. A quick stop by the supply store may take care of many classroom needs. If there is a sheet posted weekly on what is needed before the next session, specialty items can be added as well. A resourceful store manager may be able to look at the materials list of the teachers guide and provide those items requested by the teacher. A hidden supply of treats may be an added bonus.

Secret supporter

Ask parents to take turns praying for, supporting, and encouraging their child's teacher each month. Let them take the initiative to find creative (but appropriate) ways to show support.

Give 'em a break!

Intentionally plan to give teachers one Sunday a quarter off, so they can observe other teachers and learn from them. Recruit one teacher as a "floater" who rotates to classes of the grade and level where the teacher is off. Emphasize that this Sunday is for the teacher on break to be in an adult Bible class or to observe another classroom.

Alternate Plan: Have an intergenerational class or special "whole Children's Ministries" event each quarter.

Create a teacher feature

Create a regular column in your church newsletter featuring an interview or article about one of your congregation's Teachers of the Faith. Enlist student reporters too.

Apple-lause

Place a box, decorated like a large apple and labeled "Apples for the Teacher," in a prominent place in your church. Encourage members to write notes of thanks and encouragement for the various Teachers of the Faith. Share notes at a teachers meeting, then give or mail them to the teacher. For variety, you may select a particular teacher to focus on each month, with a picture and brief biography presented.

Question 2

How can our Children's Ministries be more visible and attractive in the congregation and the community?

Have a volunteer Children's Ministries publicity coordinator

The publicity coordinator's duties could include putting up posters and banners, writing articles for the local paper, taking photos, and so on.

Use a yearly theme

Establish a yearly theme, including a logo and verse, that can go on T-shirts, bookmarks, nametags, banners, the newsletter column heading, and other items where a statement about Christ's care in a quality environment can be maximized.

Suggestions:

- Shine Like Stars
- Alive in Christ
- Won by One
- Two by Two
- Jesus' Little Lambs

Make a tract or brochure

BRINGING YOUNG ONES TO JESUS

CHILI
BEANS
PEAS
TUNA
CORN

Immanuel Lutheran
   Church
123 Main St.
Anywhere, USA 12345
555-555-5555
Hector Smith, Pastor
Jane Jones, Director of
   Christian Education

Tom White, Sunday
   School Superintendent
Sally Black,
   Preschool Director
Sunday school: 9:00 A.M.
This year's Sunday school
   theme: "Bringing young
   ones to Jesus"

Rally Day: September 4
Children's Christmas service:
   7:00 P.M., Friday,
   December 23
Mission Projects:
   Community Food Pantry
   Homeless Helper Kits
   Coins for Missions

Involve children visibly in worship

- ♥ Have students perform skits illustrating the Scripture lesson or applying the lesson meaning to life.
- ♥ Include children in responsive readings (don't forget to have the leader coach them a bit).
- ♥ Have students sing for worship.
- ♥ On occasion, include students in roles often limited to adults, like greeters, choir members, ushers, acolytes.
- ♥ Have students make a project that ties into the Sunday school lessons and give it away at church.

Use your Web page potential

Make sure your Children's Ministries have an attractive page on your congregational Web site. Invite individual Sunday school classes to set up a page of their own to communicate with children their own age. Keep your Web page current and occasionally send fun, caring greetings to everyone by e-mail distribution list. Invite students to share their e-mail addresses, but also take great care to protect those addresses.

Video introduction

Make a brief take-home video with information about the church, school, Sunday school, midweek school, and teachers for distribution to people at video stores or to give to visitors. Things to include:

- Lots of footage of kids interacting and having fun
- A word of welcome from the pastor and other staff
- Comments from a happy parent and a precocious child
- Interviews with a few teachers and students
- A quick walking tour of the classroom areas
- A clip of how easy it is to register for Sunday school

Create an art gallery

Transform your most busy hallways in the building into child-made Christian craft and art galleries, which then become an opportunity for children to teach parents. Keep displays fresh and new. Find a volunteer to be the curator of the galleries.

Create television stars

Write to the local television station news anchor and offer your congregation's children for footage whenever they need something positive to say about children, education, or the church. Also offer to speak as an expert on volunteer teaching or Christian education for the news. Follow up with a phone call to the news desk editor.

Offer artwork to other "galleries"

Offer to provide or ask permission to display Sunday school art-work at the local mall or businesses. Remind the mall managers that it may bring new families into the building.

children's Ministries reports

Every time the board of education, the church council,
the voter's assembly, or any other church decision-making group
meets, offer to have a Children's Ministries report by one
or more of the children. Also take time once a month
to have a "Children's Ministries minute" as part
of the preservice announcements or at the adult Bible class.
Not only does this keep the ministry visible, it provides support
for children and helps members understand more
about their church.

Be creative, inviting the children to use a dramatization,
a puppet show, or a pantomime of one of the recent Bible stories.
Go over the presentation with the students, encouraging them
to make it as active and informational as possible.

Question 3

What can we do to help our Children's Ministries focus more on outreach to nonmembers?

Expand your visits to nursing home residents, hospital patients, and shut-ins

Many congregations have a Sunday school Christmas caroling event to a nursing home. Why not expand the care to other times of the year? Have each class adopt an individual for the whole year. Send lesson leaflets, craft projects, and pictures to your friend, and invite the person to special events in class. On Mother's or Father's Day, have children make cards and learn a few songs to share. During the summer, bring bouquets of flowers to give away. In February, build a snowman in an area visible to the person. In fall, volunteer to have students rake leaves for shut-ins. These activities give the church, its Children's Ministries, and Christ Jesus some great visibility.

Cross training

Cross' train-ing \kros' tran-ing \v. 1: to use what works to gain results 2: to employ methods from VBS to Sunday school, and vice versa 3: to use outreach ideas from secular marketing agencies

Many vacation Bible schools use a strong publicity campaign for summer enroll-ment. If it works for summer, cross over the same techniques to use for regular Sunday school or mid-week school. Door hangers, letters, personal invitations, posters, postcards, an outdoor banner, newspaper ads, and others methods can successfully be used to bring the Gospel of Christ into the lives of children.

Provide school supplies that promote your church

Make book covers, bookmarkers, imprinted pencils, or pocket notebooks with church photo and information (including address, phone number, Sunday school and worship times). Set up a booth on registration day at the beginning of the school year, and give them away or sell them for minimal costs.

Use after-school specials

Make your church a comfortable and familiar place by hosting events for kids. Schedule an event at your church after school, promoted by Sunday school children. Define an age group and target them specifically. Invite a special guest to provide magic, music, a drama, or unique games. Make sure it is well supervised, with clearly advertised beginning and ending times.

23

Be known as the "serving church"

Invite a volunteer to be in charge of arranging details for one service project each quarter. Invite families to work on it together. Projects may involve a roadside or park cleanup, a march for life, making a float in the community parade, or a number of other possibilities unique to your area.

Increase mission awareness

Recruit a mission-minded volunteer to be responsible for mission education among the children. On a regular basis, educate and celebrate God's work in other nations. Adopt a special project to support for the school year.

Have a booth at the fair

Set up a creative, active booth for your county or city fair, providing a fun and active challenge for young and old. Give away tracts about your church, balloons, and sample student materials. Let people register for a free prize, then follow up with a thank you and invitation to your church and education opportunities.

Maximize the food drive

Collect food and clothing, but rather than adding it to another agency's collection, ask the agency for addresses of those they cannot serve. Have children and families deliver the gifts. Document the activity with video or pictures for sharing later. Show it to other congregation members in a variety of settings, including meetings or Bible classes, or just before the Sunday school opening.

Open the facility for parties

Offer your church facility for Sunday birthday parties, with some suggested games and activities that a Party Volunteer Leader would organize and supervise. Encourage parents to bring their children to the party, which will include attending Sunday school and worship together, a light lunch (with a birthday cake, of course!), and games. Or permit parent-supervised sleepovers on Saturday night, allowing students to attend church and Sunday school together. Have something special that can be done in the Sunday school classroom and a list of expectations for parents wanting to use the facility.

Use creative signage

Start by having a bold outdoor sign promoting your Children's Ministries, including the logo and theme. Imagine other ways that you could improve signs. Label one entrance for Children's Ministries. Have banners out front. Paint the inside of the windows with inspiring messages that passersby can read. Make sure that a clean, neat, brightly colored building invites people in.

Question 4

How can we equip teachers with better teaching skills?

 ## Idea board

In an area where teachers usually walk, put up an idea board where they can see the text and theme of next week's lesson and begin to brainstorm ideas, writing their ideas down as they walk by. Others can piggyback on these ideas, which are less likely to be forgotten if written down.

Plan teachers meetings they'll want to attend

☆ Create a warm, inviting environment

☆ Arrive early to set up

☆ Be prepared

☆ Greet each teacher by name

☆ Provide "treats"—refreshments, small gifts, bookmarks, etc.

☆ Keep business to a minimum

☆ Be enthusiastic

☆ Hold a monthly drawing for movie passes, food coupons, a service to be donated by members, etc.

☆ Make the time meaningful spiritually— offer Bible study time

☆ Listen to teachers' concerns, needs, and interests

☆ Laugh together

☆ Provide teaching materials in advance

☆ Use teachers' skills to plan and lead sessions

Have teachers teach teachers

Rotate teachers as presenters for a portion of the teachers meeting. Use a resource like *Making a Difference* or distribute an advance copy of *Teachers Interaction* and ask a teacher to pick a meaningful article to share with other teachers. Provide additional copies of *Teachers Interaction* and highlighters for everyone in attendance.

Budget for growth opportunities

You may "have not because you ask not." Request budget money to send a certain number of teachers to specialized conferences and workshops for Teachers of the Faith and other Children's Ministries. Some events will be more expensive than others, but most should be meaningful. Sending teachers on a road trip affirms them as persons and thanks them for their gift of service to Christ and your church. Don't wait for an event to be advertised first; budget *now*, and carry over funds to a future year with a more expensive trip, if needed.

Broaden your people resources

You probably have many people in the congregation who may be willing to serve as resources to help develop teaching, group, and staff skills:

- A physician or nurse
- A mental health counselor
- A police officer
- A university professor
- The manager of a business catering to children
- An advertising executive
- A performer (musician, artist, storyteller)
- A member of the school district staff
- An electronics store worker

Make staff evaluations fun!

Meet at a place and time that is less threatening, in a casual setting.

Characteristics for teaching staff:

Joyfully lives out the Christian faith

Is a healthy role model of the Christian faith

Is positive about the church and their part in the Children's Ministry

Has a functional understanding of Law and Gospel

Incorporates a variety of techniques to enhance learning

Relates well with students

Relates well with parents and families

Uses good classroom management techniques

Attends meetings and training events

Comes to class prepared

Works well with others on the staff

Is able to witness and train others to share the faith

Is flexible

Characteristics for nonteaching staff:

Understands the role

Is prompt and punctual

Is positive about the Children's Ministries programs

Gets along well with children; is appropriate

Willingly volunteers to help with a project

Carries through on commitments

Communicates well: listens carefully, asks questions, and speaks up when necessary

Models the Christian lifestyle

Develop a mentor program

Team a new teacher with a veteran teacher to bring rich benefits to both. Encourage them to use the following discussion questions, and purchase local coffee shop coupons as a way to encourage them to sit down once each quarter and share their thoughts and reflections. Mentor programs generally work better when the novice selects his or her own mentor. Remind veteran teachers of the positive benefits they can enjoy through mentoring.

What gives you the most joy in teaching?

HMMM... I WONDER? ? ?

What new strategy did you try this quarter?

What would you like to learn more about?

What is your favorite Bible story to teach?

How do you prepare your lesson material?

Eat one bite at a time

By trying one new skill or idea each month, you will gradually become better at a whole range of skills. How do you eat an elephant? One bite at a time!

- Begin preparations a week before class
- Carry your standard supplies in a fishing tackle box or makeup case
- Have a volunteer organize extra leaflet covers and other artwork by Bible story
- Use a highlighter to prepare your lesson plan
- Find creative ways to do the end-of-lesson review
- Invite the children's choir to make a tape of your favorite songs to sing
- Involve a different parent each week to be your teacher aide
- Learn and review the same memory passage all month long
- Have one student each week volunteer to sharpen pencils, clean the chalkboard, and do other miscellaneous tasks

Maximize your resource library

If you don't have a resource library, start with a few key resources and gradually add to your collection. Make sure it is easily accessible, in a location that teachers frequent. Begin with a good concordance, Bible dictionary, and Bible atlas. As time goes on, add a one-volume commentary or a user-friendly series for teachers, like The People's Bible Commentary. Later, add some teacher resource books with memory games, crossword puzzles, coloring pages, and other resources. Add sparingly and carefully. Highlight a book of the month, with a special endorsement by the pastor, superintendent, or revered teacher.

CROSSWORD PUZZLES! BIBLE ATLAS!

ARCHY'S CHRISTIAN BOOK FAIR TODAY!

Memory Games & Coloring Pages

BIBLE DICTIONARY

LOOK WHAT'S NEW

Host a book fair

Book fair hosts have access to great resources and receive book incentives and benefits for hosting. Add to your collection of teaching, professional, church library, and children's books.

Call 1-800-779-0846 for more information!

Question 5

What are some great ways to maximize the teaching hour?

Use the 160-hour rule

Do the math. Twenty-four hours a day times seven days a week between Sunday school classes, minus the hour of class, equals 167 hours. On Sunday, after you've taught and worshiped in the morning, allow yourself the afternoon to relax and enjoy the day of rest. Before you go to bed on Sunday night, brief yourself on the Bible story and truths you'll be teaching the next Sunday. Scan the teachers guide for an hour or less. This 160-hour advance notice gives you several benefits.

- You won't get a Saturday night surprise.

- With the story in the back of your mind, you will pick up related ideas and thoughts throughout the week that will help the lesson come alive.

- Preparation time will be cut as you pick up needed materials and supplies during your regular weekly routine.

A few minutes each evening, throughout the week, creates a more thoughtful time of preparation. This routine will help you feel more confident that you are at your best on Sunday morning.

So start today. At C – 160, begin the countdown to class time.

Use the 10-minute rule

If you have a one-hour class, plan for it as if it were six 10-minute units. When the teachers guide suggests a longer time for an activity, subdivide the activity into smaller parts and introduce variety into that component. Consider relocating for some of those units, as necessary or appropriate. Use the five senses as a checklist to see if you are including variety. Some of the units can be teacher focused, others student focused; some can be active, others can be passive. Organized variety enhances the class experience.

Think hook, book, look

Whether you have 30 minutes or three hours in the classroom, plan deliberate time to (1) "hook" or grab the students' attention when you introduce the Bible theme; (2) spend time in God's "book," the source of our teaching about Jesus Christ, the Savior; and (3) "look" at how the Bible story is applied in the daily life of the students.

Time it out

⋙▷ Music time

⋙▷ Puppets tell the story

⋙▷ Craft activity

⋙▷ Memory work

⋙▷ Lesson reinforcement activity

Too often, time runs short in the classroom. Expect that you will never get it all said. However, you need to plan carefully to ensure that the main priorities of the class are covered. To keep you on track, jot down in the teachers guide the time in the classroom hour when each event takes place. Overplan, but have them be subordinate to the main points. Or, make sticky notes and tape them to the clock for the beginning of each activity. Students will help keep you on track too.

Plan your transitions

We may spend so much time planning the meat of the lesson that we forget our transitions. If transitions are poorly executed, students may disconnect from the content and fail to see how the introductory activity applies to the Bible story or how the Bible story applies to their life. Write a brief transition sentence on a sticky pad for each time that you shift gears. Find the art of making a good connection and use it to segue into the next point. Repeating the main point or focus statement of the lesson is often a helpful basis for transitions.

MEMORY

CRAFT

SMOOTH TRANSITIONS

Use these tips for healthy discipline

BE ORGANIZED

BE RESPECTFUL

BE FIRM

BE FAIR

BE PROMPT

Be proactive in relationship building

Be sure to know at least one bit of personal information about every child in your class.

It may be helpful to know that

- Alex loves to play soccer, and his dad coaches his team;
- Anne has a dollhouse that her grandfather made for her.

Take time to find out about the individual student:

- Listen to what students say *and* what they don't say.
- Ask about their interests on a regular basis.
- Comment on their clothing, through which they can tell you a lot about themselves.

Use Purposeful Active Learning

Use active learning techniques that have a purpose and clearly relate to the Bible story. Remember that "active learning" means that the brain is activated rather than just that the body is moving. Active learning can be highly interactive and may seem less controlled, but can be shaped for a great learning experience.

The Active Learning Cycle

Do It (experience an activity)

Publish It (talk about what happened)

Process It (ask "why" and "what does this teach us" questions)

Generalize (ask, "what does this mean for others or for us at another time?")

Apply (discuss what ways this new information can be applied to real life)

Have COWs in your Sunday school

Place a bulletin board in a highly visible area. On it, feature a "**C**lass **o**f the **W**eek" and a "**C**hild **o**f the **W**eek." Feature them with a photo and some words describing the child or the class, as well as words from the child or the class describing what Jesus, the church, and Sunday school mean to them. Find a group or organization to sponsor a special treat for the **COW**s each week.

Emphasize Christ in every lesson

✝ Look for Christ as you study and prepare.

✝ Point out Jesus *in the text* as you teach the lesson.

✝ Emphasize Jesus as the living, loving, forgiving Savior, not merely an example for behavior.

✝ Make sure the summary and focus emphasizes Christ.

Delegate to motivate

Many students want to do more than just show up for class. Involve students in a meaningful way that helps you with your tasks.

Assign students different tasks such as these that are rotated on a weekly or monthly basis:

Welcomers

Attendance keepers

Setup or cleanup

Acolytes

Offering collector

Story time helper

Prayer leader

Snack provider

Music helper

Peer-care helper

Allow the students to suggest other ways that they can help in your classroom.

Question 6

How can we get parents to support the Children's Ministries and other church activities, including adult Bible class?

Send a letter of introduction

At the beginning of the school year or class cycle, have each teacher send a photo and letter of introduction to the parents of each child in the class. Teachers should include a brief note about their background, experience, and goals, as well as a pledge to work with parents to nurture their children in the faith.

Dear Mr. and Mrs. Shaw,

Hi! My name is Ms. Lopez. I will be Anna's teacher in Sunday school. Together we will learn about "Our Life in Christ." Jesus wants us to learn more about Him, and regular attendance at Sunday school and church nurtures Anna's faith. You will also grow in faith and set a good Christian example by attending church and Bible class. Together you, Anna, and I will learn of the love of God for us in Christ.

I will be praying for you and for Anna. Please let me know if there are any special concerns that you want me to include. Visit with me about any special circumstances you want to share or if you have any great ideas for ministry with your family.

In Christ,

Ms. Lopez

Ms. Lopez

Sunday School Parent Covenant

God has given parents the responsibility for the spiritual welfare and eternal salvation of their children. This responsibility leads parents to bring their children to Christ and His church for Holy Baptism. The church then agrees to partner with, but not replace, parents in the spiritual nurture of their children. Sunday school and other Children's Ministries supplement what God desires to take place in the home.

Parent's Commitment

- I agree to pray for my child on a regular basis.
- I agree to set an example of the Christian lifestyle by being involved regularly in worship at church.
- I agree to set an example of Christian nurture by being involved in a Bible study.
- I agree to make every attempt to live as Christ would lead me, rejoicing in His forgiveness whenever I fail and offering forgiveness to my child as necessary.
- I agree to share Bible stories and devotional thoughts with my child.
- I agree to teach my child the basics of Christian prayer.
- I agree to bring my child regularly to worship and Sunday school.
- I agree to enroll my child in confirmation class and other growth opportunities.
- I agree to support the staff of the church's educational ministry in whatever ways possible, and will consider my role as a classroom helper or teacher.
- I agree to support the work of my church with my time, my talents and abilities, and my money.

Church's Commitment

- We agree to offer regular worship services for you to attend.
- We agree to offer a variety of Bible study opportunities for your participation.
- We agree to use a portion of your donated monies to provide staff, materials, and resources for the Christian education of your child.
- We agree to teach the truths of the Bible according to the beliefs of our church body.
- We invite you to share your questions, concerns, and ideas with us.
- We welcome your involvement in our educational ministry.
- We agree to keep our classroom open, so you may visit and sit in at any time.
- We promise to love your child and share the truths of God's love and forgiveness from the Bible.

Send puppets home

If the students in your class get excited about a puppet character telling the story each week, allow students to rotate the chance for taking the puppet home. Make sure they and their parents understand the importance of bringing the puppet back to class the next week, but be prepared just in case. Encourage students and parents to use the puppet for devotions each night, retelling the Bible story. Back in class, allow students to tell about the adventures they and the puppet shared during the week.

Offer classes for parents

If you offer a variety of classes for parents, keep them Christ-centered and Bible-based; locate them near where the youngest children are in Sunday school. Create relationships between parents, and challenge them to sponsor projects for the Sunday school. Use the class as a mentoring place for new teachers.

Print a parents newsletter

A newsletter dedicated to parenting can emphasize the priority of families and parenting in your congregation. Reproducible content pages are available from the Lutheran Family Association, 3558 S. Jefferson, St. Louis, MO 63118. Additional content may be gotten from *Teachers Interaction* magazine or the *Superintendent's Helper* planning guide. A calendar and personal notes from the superintendent or a particular teacher will enhance the value of the newsletter.

Create a parents handbook

Here's a sample of a possible Table of Contents page.

Who we are
What we believe
The mission of our church
The purpose of our Children's Ministry program
Meet the church staff
Meet the Sunday school superintendent
Meet the Sunday school teachers
The goals for Sunday school
Addressing discipline issues
Our open classrooms
What parents can expect from us
What we expect of parents
Connecting the Sunday school and the home
Dealing with your questions and concerns
Maps of the campus
Our yearly schedule
Registration forms
How to get involved

Promote family devotions

Set up a devotional center with donated or purchased items. One week, have each student bring a small suitcase or tote bag and select things they want to use for family devotions. Promote the idea with parents, so the process does not surprise them. Have students return their bag the next week and exchange it for someone else's bag, or restock the devotion center and let students pick a new assortment of items for their devotions that week.

Start early

Initiate a Sunday school class for two-year-olds and their parents in the classroom together. Both groups will benefit from learning the routine, and growing together. The teacher's task will be to enable the parents to work independently with their child.

Consider the *Together with Jesus* curriculum from CPH as a great start for these classes.

Host a parent/grandparent month

Rather than a single day, designate a whole month for parents and grandparents to visit the classroom. Parents with conflicting work schedules or who have many children involved in the church's Children's Ministries will be better accommodated. Remind students without grandparents close by to "adopt" someone special to visit. If necessary, recruit some willing senior citizens to "adopt" students; encourage them to continue the friendship after Grandparent Month.

Calling all parents and grandparents

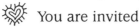 You are invited

 As a special guest

In your (grand) son or daughter's Sunday school classroom

Any Sunday this month.

No RSVP required.

Come prepared to participate and join in the fun of knowing Jesus!

Show parents that they are special

Parent involvement checklist

❀ Have home visit with parents

❀ Use parents as greeters

❀ Post a list of important tasks that parents could sign up for

❀ Invite parents to rotate as room parents in their child's classroom

❀ Use a parent as a mystery guest each week to play a game, review the story, or pass out a treat

TREATS

HELLO!

THIS SUNDAY'S MYSTERY GUEST IS......?

Use an outline for home visits

Make an appointment ahead of time

Bring a photo album of the classroom to show to the family

Gather the family and ask them to complete these sentences:
- The best part of Sunday school is …
- My favorite memory from Sunday school is …
- My favorite Sunday school song is …
- My favorite Bible story is …

Be prepared to briefly retell a familiar Bible story and have an activity for the family to do together

Ask a few questions about the story

Ask for prayer requests, close with prayer

Invite parents or students to ask any questions

Leave some sample leaflets, a tape, or a bookmark

Remind them of any special upcoming events

VACATION BIBLE SCHOOL JUNE 12-16 $10.00

Consider a registration fee

Consider having a registration fee for involvement in the Children's Ministries programs. People may place greater value on what they pay for. This may gain their support in other areas as well. Remind families that this does not take the place of their regular stewardship practices.

Question 7

How can we better plan and implement special events into our Children's Ministries?

Rehearsal for "Jesus Lights the Way"
1:30–2:30 P.M. (promptly)

Preschoolers and Kindergartners meet in chapel

Grades 1–3 meet in the fellowship hall

Grades 4–6 meet in the sanctuary

Grades 7–8 meet in the youth room

Parents' class meets in the library

Drop-off baby-sitting (for parents who want to go shopping) is in the nursery

Maximize rehearsal times

☆ Begin your preparations as early as possible; six months ahead is not too soon.

☆ Minimize the "wait" time by meeting in smaller groups to rehearse, then gathering the whole group for a half hour.

☆ Have a clear picture of what will happen, and write scripted notes. Much time is wasted when the director is not prepared for movement and stage directions.

☆ Involve older youth by having them sit with the classes or especially antsy children.

☆ Offer a class or activity for parents during the rehearsal time. (Consider having other activities for the children on one Sunday to allow parents time for shopping or holiday preparations.)

51

Create a six-month special events calendar

Distribute the calendar liberally.

Hold a "Trunk or Treat" activity in the church parking lot

Invite volunteers, families, or church groups to set up "trunks" of candy, tracts, or small prizes in the church parking lot for Halloween. Decorate, avoiding non-Christian themes. Include one trunk with information about your church and Children's Ministries.

Get creative with family activities

Gather some creative folks in a room. Take 10 minutes to share your goals for the meeting: to brainstorm possible themes and events for family ministry. Let the group brainstorm for 15 minutes, tossing out ideas without interruption for evaluation. Then take five minutes to select which ones to work on for the next year. Invite volunteers to organize one of the events. Here are some idea starters:

- **Marty Party** (for Martin Luther's birthday, November 10)
- **"Souper" Bowl party** at a local soup kitchen
- **"Grounded in Grace"** theme on Groundhog's Day

Be creative with the use of time

- After school
- Week nights
- Saturday mornings
- Days off school
- The off-peak hours on a holiday
- Short time slots, rather than large
- Over Sunday dinner
- Friday night family night
- Weekend "matinee" hours

Keep "special events" special

Avoid devaluing the term "special" by working through this checklist before repeating any successful program. You might do this shortly after the event and again when the planning team meets to consider repeating the activity.

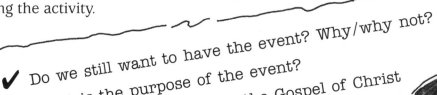

✔ Do we still want to have the event? Why/why not?

✔ What is the purpose of the event?

✔ How does the event bring the Gospel of Christ to people?

✔ What new twist can we add to the event?

✔ What other event might accomplish our goal in a better way?

✔ What components of the activity are important to keep? What can be changed?

✔ Is this the best time of year to have the event? When would it be better?

✔ How can our publicity capitalize on the unique strengths of this program?

Learn from discount chain stores

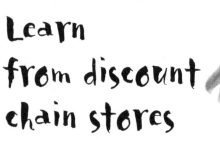

Invite retirement-age folks to be greeters at significant points throughout the building. They can direct students and parents, as well as spread good cheer and the love of Christ. Ask them to visit one class to affirm the teacher and students when their shift ends. Staffing with multiple greeters allows a greeter to personally escort visitors to their destination, explaining more about the church en route.

Target inactive children

Plan, publicize, and promote special events that may appeal to inactive children. Rather than minimizing the Bible study/lesson time, enhance it. Examples:

Costume Day

Popcorn Day

Picture Day
(to be taken at church)

Photo-Sharing Day
(bring five favorite photos to tell about yourself)

Show-and-Tell Day

Video Day
(watch *Prince of Egypt,* etc.)

Host a "Values Night"

Before the event, publicize it as a values dinner and evening. Charge a minimal cost to cover expenses for a good meal; donate the proceeds to a local or international hunger campaign. Ask each person *and* each family to bring something to symbolize what is most valuable to them. Begin the evening with a third-world banquet. Serve one third of the people pizza, hamburgers, spaghetti, or another traditional American meal. Serve another third of the people rice or beans only. The last third receives a hot, weak, broth with no meat.

Discuss how each person felt in the process.

Discuss how our values might be different than people from other parts of the world.

Have persons share their valuable items in small groups.

Ask the whole group, "What do these things indicate about our values system?"

Have families or small groups do a character analysis of someone in the Bible, listing positive and negative values.

Have families or small groups develop a collage depicting positive values. Have each group share their thoughts with the large group. Post them for everyone to see.

Emphasize the value of family as a place for faith conversation and development. Underscore each person's value to God, demonstrated in the sacrifice of Jesus for us.

Use congregational drama

Consider a series of family-led or small-group-performed one-act plays, or select a performance that can be done well without intense rehearsals and staging expectations. Publicize throughout the area. Afterwards, have the actors visit the Sunday school classrooms. Have the church staff or evangelism committee members visit nonmembers for follow up.

(Consider *Fearless Pharaoh FooFoo and Other Dramas for Children* [CPH 1998] as an excellent drama resource.)

PRINT!
CUT!
DANISH!
COFFEE!
ACTION!
CAMERA!
LIGHTS!

SCRIPT

DIRECTOR

I'M READY FOR MY CLOSE-UP, MR. DEMILLE

SCENE 1 TAKE 86

How can we recruit and equip substitute teachers for a successful class experience?

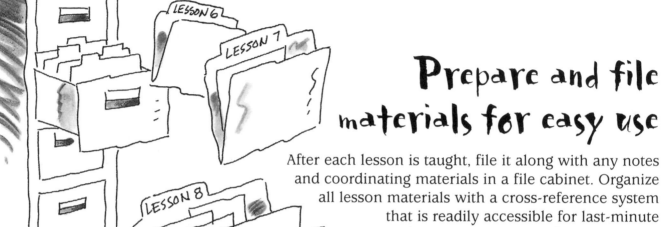

Prepare and file materials for easy use

After each lesson is taught, file it along with any notes and coordinating materials in a file cabinet. Organize all lesson materials with a cross-reference system that is readily accessible for last-minute substitutes. Have some favorite lessons for combined and intergenerational classes available as well.

Activate your substitutes

Rather than calling upon a substitute only when there is an actual vacancy, bring the substitute into the classroom early in the year as a team teacher. If things go well and the substitute is willing, schedule the substitute for team teaching responsibilities on an occasional or regular basis. This helps both the substitute and the class by building relationships and clearing up expectations early. Substitutes may be easier to recruit if they know the specific grade they will be asked to teach.

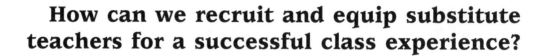

Give first-class treatment to substitutes

Treat substitute teachers with the same honor, respect, and favor as regular teachers and helpers. Encourage, train, recognize, and affirm them and their commitment to the ministry of Jesus Christ. Don't overlook cookie bakers, flower providers, snack preparers, craft helpers, attendance keepers, music leaders, and others who use their talents and gifts to serve Christ and work toward building up the Kingdom of God.

Match substitutes in teams

Rather than putting one person in a classroom as a substitute, match two compatible people as a substitute team. This allows for better classroom management in a strange environment.

Substitutes

Have someone ready on stand-by

Ask a volunteer to prepare a drama or presentation that could be used in any age classroom and done without a lot of lead time. The same substitute can thoroughly prepare once to teach the same lesson in a number of different classes, especially if it is a lesser-known Bible account or story about a church hero.

Have teachers teach their class how to treat a substitute teacher

Introduce yourselves.

Remember the substitute's feelings.

Treat the substitute teacher as you would like to be treated.

Treat the substitute as you think Jesus might treat her.

Be polite.

Help the teacher with unfamiliar issues.

Remember that classroom rules still apply.

Train your substitutes

In addition to providing your substitutes with the same training as your regular teachers, give these pointers for leading a one-session class:

🍎 Invite a parent to be in the classroom with you.

🍎 Spend time introducing yourself.

🍎 Get to know the students.

🍎 Have a lesson plan clearly in mind, and follow it even if it is different from the class tradition.

🍎 Don't compete with the regular teacher.

🍎 Don't let yourself be intimidated by the image of the perfect teacher. No one is that person.

🍎 Be firm but fair.

🍎 Don't be afraid to discipline.

Use "Pick-up Paks"

Have a master teacher prepare two or three lessons that are ready to use and easily accessible, so that when there is no time for preparation, a substitute teacher can select the story he or she wants and walk into the classroom prepared to teach the lesson for the day. A great resource is to take a few of the best VBS lessons and save them for inclusion in the Sunday or midweek school year.

JESUS DIED FOR ME

DAVID & GOLIATH

LESSONS 1-5 GRADES 3-6

LESSONS 10-11

NOAH & THE ARK

JESUS' BIRTH

JESUS WALKS ON WATER

CARD GAME

GRADES 3-6

LESSON #12

JESUS TAKES CARE OF ME

EARLY CHILDHOOD

Use a job description for your substitute teachers

**Job Description
for Substitute Teachers of the Faith**

In order to serve our Lord through His children of this congregation in the best way possible, all substitute Teachers of the Faith should meet these requirements:

- Be a regular worshiper and Bible student.
- Pray regularly for the Sunday school program, staff, students, and teachers.
- Provide telephone numbers for contact, and indicate how much advance time you need.
- Indicate the preferred age levels for whom you would substitute.
- Be willing to attend a teachers meeting to prepare you for the Sunday you need to teach.
- Be willing to attend a training session for teachers and/or substitutes.
- Entrust the class time to the Lord's direction.

EMPLOYMENT OFFICE

JOB DESCRIPTION

JOB RESUME

Plan for a positive beginning

Have the superintendent come into the classroom and introduce the substitute teacher and stay long enough for student introductions. The superintendent can firmly review the rules and expectations for students and the classroom hour. As the superintendent leaves, he or she can remind the students, "I'll check back after a few minutes." Students who know the superintendent is returning may be more likely to make it a good transition for the substitute. Make "sub Sundays" special for teachers and kids. You may even give a coupon for "sub" sandwiches to students after they have had a good class with a substitute teacher.

Question 9

How can we maximize our facility when space is at a premium?

Carefully evaluate your facility

During the height of activity, take time to walk through your facility and carefully evaluate the groups using each location. Consider these questions:

✔ Is sound an issue?

✔ What access needs exist for that class?

✔ What is the class size?

✔ How flexible is the teacher?

Share your findings and ideas at your next teachers meeting. Pool the collective resources of the group. Make every attempt to match class needs with room possibilities. Don't be afraid to relocate classes to the most appropriate location.

Use "borrowed" or "shared" space

Use hallways, the narthex, an elevator waiting area, or another part of the building for more active parts of the lesson. Even the boiler room can be useable for classroom space if adequate measures are taken to ensure student safety.

Match a classroom to its use

Offer a class for parents in a location adjacent to where the very young children are holding class. A room with a curtain may be useable (even though it is distracting) for parents who are used to multiple children. Insecure children also have easy access to their parents this way.

Locate a class for older adults in close proximity to the active Sunday school classes

Sometimes people don't support building projects or remodeling because they aren't aware of the need for expanded space. Rather than catering to the adult comfort level, let adults "live in the trenches"; they'll likely suggest and support an education-wing addition after they've seen the need firsthand.

It's all in a name

If your room is awkward or inadequate, don't complain about it—make the most of it. Begin by letting the students suggest a creative name for the room or a part of the room. Decorate a windowless room with animal pictures and call it "the ark." If you're in the kitchen, go every week to the refrigerator for the "cool" project of the day or look in there for the "bread of life." Gather students in a circle on a floor next to the only solid "Bible Wall" in a room where three walls are curtains.

67

Create a "safe" environment wherever you are

DISPOSABLE WIPES

TAPE

GAUZE

SOFT HANDS LOTION

BAND-AGES

INDUCES VOMITING IN POISONING CASES

ANTIBACTERIAL OINTMENT

EYE FLUSH CUP

SYRUP OF IPECAC

SUN BLOCK

PLASTIC FISHING TACKLE BOX

PAIN KILLER

ALOE VERA GEL

STOMACH CALM

CHILDREN'S FIRST AID

FIRST-AID KIT
A well-supplied first-aid kit should be easily accessible to Sunday School teachers and staff, but inaccessible to young students.

Adjust the lesson plan to the room and the room for your lesson plan

As you look at your lesson plan, ask what ways your seating structure and classroom design may be able to enhance the lesson. For example, a semi-circle may work well where eye contact is important to maintain discipline; an open floor space may be necessary for a large group activity. Rows are rarely necessary, but may be a helpful variant to the classroom design.

Keep your ideas cool

If you share a space with a day school class and want to create a separate classroom within the classroom, get a large refrigerator box from an appliance store. Lay it on its side, and use it as a small Bible study or activity area for part of the classroom time. If there is space, use it for class storage during the week. Let the students decorate it periodically, and replace it whenever necessary. It can be easily folded up for storage and brought out for class time each week.

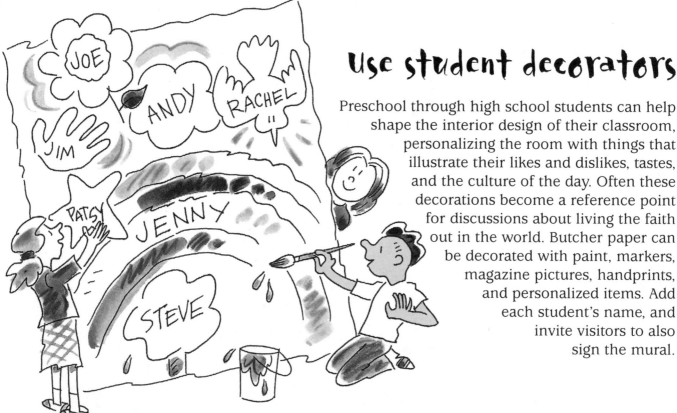

Use student decorators

Preschool through high school students can help shape the interior design of their classroom, personalizing the room with things that illustrate their likes and dislikes, tastes, and the culture of the day. Often these decorations become a reference point for discussions about living the faith out in the world. Butcher paper can be decorated with paint, markers, magazine pictures, handprints, and personalized items. Add each student's name, and invite visitors to also sign the mural.

Communicate the Sunday school mission

The goal of Immanuel Sunday school is to help students be

Rooted in God's word,
Growing in the Christian faith,
Branching out to share the love of Christ,
Bearing the fruit of faith.

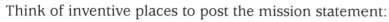

Think of inventive places to post the mission statement:

- ☺ On bulletin boards in the building
- ☺ In the church newsletter
- ☺ In the Sunday school brochure
- ☺ On bookmarks
- ☺ On a banner above the superintendent's door
- ☺ At the entrance to each classroom
- ☺ On a banner in church

Use creative storage space

If there is no storage space in the classroom, create your own "cupboards" using inexpensive plastic storage containers with sealable lids. Activity center supplies can be kept in them, as can extra resources, magazines for cutting apart, and other miscellaneous supplies. Even Bibles can be contained there.

Decorate creatively

If bulletin boards are not available, give teachers access to sheets of plywood, Masonite, or even water-resistant shower or decorative wallboard to create portable bulletin boards that can be personalized for the class. You may wish to cover the boards with a bedsheet, to which you can attach items with pins. Let students decorate the bulletin boards as part of the review of the lesson each week. Let the board be a "communication board" of what students learned during class.

What are some things a superintendent can do to help recruit teachers and to have fun doing other miscellaneous tasks?

Use a standard Teacher of the Faith job description

Teacher of the Christian Faith Job Description

1. Teachers of the Faith are important members of the ministry team at _____ Church because of their direct contact and influence with the children and other members of this congregation.

2. Teachers of the Faith are appointed to their positions by the Board of Christian Education on the recommendation of the superintendent of the education programs and with the approval of the pastor or elders. They are appointed to their positions for a period not to exceed one year.

3. Teachers of the Faith are to consider prayerfully each lesson they prepare to teach. They are to regard highly the spiritual needs of the people entrusted to their care.

4. Teachers of the Faith will strive to teach in ways that will promote the spiritual health and nurture of their students.

5. Teachers of the Faith are to pray continually for their students and for the success of the children's ministry.

6. Teachers of the Faith will faithfully attend all training sessions and staff meetings offered for their benefit.

7. Teachers of the Faith are to arrive in their classroom at least 15 minutes prior to the beginning of the session.

8. Teachers of the Faith, in cooperation with the superintendent, are to minister to those students who attend irregularly.

9. Teachers of the Faith, as their time permits, are to supervise their students as they participate in additional activities such as singing for a worship service or working in a service project.

10. Teachers of the Faith are to be friends and counselors to their students. If feasible, teachers should visit the homes of their students and use every means possible to establish rapport with them and their family members.

Qualifications:

☆ Is a strong Christian with a passion for Jesus Christ.

☆ Possesses a love for children and their families.

☆ Is able to effectively communicate.

☆ Is willing to commit time to preparation, meetings, and class experience.

Carefully recruit

Stop

Carefully reflect on the priorities, needs, and goals of the Children's Ministry.

Caringly visit with the pastor, and review the membership list.

Look

Carefully search for candidates who are already students of the Word in Bible class and are regular in worship.

Carefully look for high energy, a love for Jesus, the ability to communicate, and flexibility.

Listen

Carefully listen to what is being said and not said: objections, concerns, and ideas.

Listen carefully to needs and preferences of future teachers.

Speak

Caringly ask if they will serve Christ and His Church, as well as His children.

Caringly assure teachers that you and the rest of the church stand behind them.

Desperation is destructive. Avoid begging in the newsletter, the bulletin, or other publications. Avoid using guilt, peer pressure, threats to discontinue the program, or other manipulative tactics. Don't whine or complain. Speak as positively as possible, and seek positive and dedicated, enthusiastic staff. Set high standards, and let God provide people to fill the needs.

Prayerfully recruit

It is God's will that children learn of Christ. We can and should pray boldly and confidently for God's direction and blessing. Places to include petitions that God would send and equip teachers for your Children's Ministries:

- 😊 in worship prayers
- 😊 on the prayer chain
- 😊 at small group meetings
- 😊 during Sunday school opening
- 😊 at organizational meetings around church
- 😊 at home
- 😊 at a special prayer vigil for education ministries

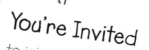

You're Invited

to join us in prayer for our Sunday school

Who: You

When: Daily at 9 A.M.

Where: At work, home, in your car, at the ballpark, anywhere and everywhere

Why: God invites us to pray and promises to hear what we pray

How: "Dear God, our Children's Ministry belongs to You. Show us, lead us, and strengthen us for what You have planned for us here in our congregation. Direct our educational leaders (list them by name). Raise up volunteers for our Sunday school to share Jesus using the gifts You have given them. God, bring people of all ages to our education program—children, teens, and adults—so all can learn to know You. In the name of Jesus we pray. Amen.

74

More is better

We like to keep things simple, and sometimes it is easier to do things oneself than to have unreliable help. Working alone takes less time (at first), and you have fewer surprises. However, when you try to balance everything, you are more likely to drop something.

Recruit more teachers, parents, and grandparents for limited, short-term responsibilities. People are more likely to become involved if they clearly understand their task and know how much time is involved. The more limited the task, the easier it is to recruit.

Personal testimony

Remind your current staff to take every opportunity to share the positive things that happen in your church's Children's Ministries. More conversation increases awareness. The more time you spend extolling the virtues, successes, and directions of the children's ministry, the more people are apt to become involved. Recruitment is easier if there is already a positive image of what people are being asked to be part of.

Use these venues to talk positively about your Children's Ministries:

- In the family
- With neighbors and friends
- At church meetings
- In front of the congregation

Teachers of the Faith hit list

Keep a running list of prospective Children's Ministries volunteers.
Look for them everywhere:

TEACHERS HIT LIST

- ✔ In the drive-by/drop-off lane before and after church (parents)
- ✔ At family activity events
- ✔ In the worship service
- ✔ In the adult Bible class
- ✔ Among the older teenagers and young adults
- ✔ Amidst senior citizens and grandparents
- ✔ In the professional classroom
- ✔ From among health service professionals
- ✔ On a tractor
- ✔ In the repair shop
- ✔ In a human resources department

Use a medical release form

Sample Medical Release Form

Child's Name _____

Home Address _____

_____

_____

Parent or Guardian _____

    Home Phone _____ Work Phone _____

Child's Doctor _____

    Office Phone _____

Child's Dentist _____

    Office Phone _____

Preferred Hospital _____

Emergency Contacts:

Person _____

    Relation: _____ Phone no. _____

Person: _____

    Relation: _____ Phone no. _____

Other Pertinent Information _____

_____

_____

_____

_____

Parent's Signature _____

Date _____

Superintendent's checklist

Facility and Space Issues

☐ Room Assignments

☐ Heating/cooling adjustments, windows, fans (weekly)

☐ Tables, chairs, desks, carpet, pillows

☐ Blackboard, chalk, eraser or whiteboard and markers

☐ Locking/unlocking rooms

☐ Lights

☐ AV equipment

Materials and Supplies

☐ Teachers guides, teachers packets, student leaflets, student packets

☐ Bibles, pencils/pens, blank paper, markers, crayons, scissors, construction paper, tape, glue

☐ Additional resources (puzzles, coloring pages, memory guides)

Recruitment and retention

Number of teachers _____

Number of teaching assistants _____

Number of parent helpers _____

Opening devotion leader _____

Musician _____

☐ Issue "Call to Teach"

☐ Personally contact all candidates

☐ Remember staff birthdays

☐ Notes of encouragement and thanks

Reporting

☐ Record attendance

☐ Record offering

☐ Update file on each student/family

☐ Track absence streaks

☐ Follow-up notes to visitors

☐ Permission slips for any special events

Publicity

☐ Bulletin

☐ Monthly church newsletter

☐ Special events for local paper

Meetings

☐ Board of education

☐ Quarterly meeting with the pastor

☐ Weekly, biweekly, or monthly teachers meetings (prepare brief agenda)

☐ Quarterly teachers fellowship event

The most important things for me to do today:

1. _____

2. _____

3. _____

Personal letter

Dear Jennifer,

Hello! I hope you are having a good spring, enjoying the warmer weather and new leaves.

Last Sunday, when the Sunday school children sang in church, I noticed the intent look and the loving, caring smile on your face that reflected through your eyes. It appears that you really enjoy children and also deeply love Jesus, your Savior.

Next fall we will be looking for a few selected individuals to help with some Sunday school responsibilities. As you know, the Children's Ministries are very important to our congregation. We strive to share the love of Jesus Christ with each child and want to provide additional opportunities to share with them. You have been carefully and prayerfully considered, with the approval of the pastor and the boards of elders and education. I will follow up with a telephone call or personal conversation to explain more about what role you might play and what you might expect as a staff member. Please pray with me that God would lead you to a comfortable decision of service to Him.

In Christ,

Superintendent

Bob

Don't forget to follow up with a phone call or personal contact within five days of mailing the letter!

My teaching covenant

Having been rescued by my Lord and Savior, Jesus Christ, from sin, death, and the power of the devil and restored to an eternal life that began at Holy Baptism, I feel led by God's Spirit to serve as a Teacher of the Faith. To that end, I commit to the following:

☆ I will continue my regular devotional Bible reading and prayer times.

☆ I will continue in my contact with the Word and Sacrament ministry of the church, being regular in worship and Bible study.

☆ I will attend regular teachers meetings.

☆ I will participate in the staff training sessions.

☆ I will actively prepare my lesson plans and invest myself in preparation for the weekly hour of teaching.

☆ I will pray for the spiritual growth and development of my students.

☆ I expect my congregation to uphold me in the following ways:

　❤ Offer opportunities for my spiritual growth and development.

　❤ Provide Christ-centered, Bible based, life-directed curricular resources.

　❤ Pray for my educational task and me.

　❤ Support my ideas for ministry to the children and their families.

　❤ Provide adequate facilities for the class.

　❤ Remember that I am out of the loop on some issues because of my commitment, and keep me informed and aware of other ministry issues.

Signed _____

Date _____

Signed _____

Signed _____

SIGNED, SEALED & DELIVERED